Reading Games
with Ziggy the Zebra

Second Edition

by
Marie Rippel

All About Reading
Level 1 Supplement

All rights reserved. No portion of this publication may be reproduced by any means, including duplicating, photocopying, electronic, mechanical, recording, the World Wide Web, e-mail, or otherwise, without written permission from the publisher.

Copyright © 2016, 2012 by All About® Learning Press, Inc.
Printed in the United States of America

All About® Learning Press, Inc.
615 Commerce Loop
Eagle River, WI 54521

ISBN 978-1-935197-68-3

v. 2.0.0

Editor: Renée LaTulippe
Contributors: Renée LaTulippe and Samantha Johnson
Illustrator: Mike Eustis
Cover and Page Design: Dave LaTulippe

Reading Games with Ziggy the Zebra is part of the
All About® Reading program.

For more books in this series, go to www.AllAboutReading.com.

Contents

1 Preparing for Takeoff

Correlation with *All About Reading* Level 1 .... **7**

Meet Ziggy! **9**

Map of Ziggy's Travels **13**

How to Make the File Folder Games **19**

Who Goes First? **21**

2 Up and Away!

Game 1: Apples for Ziggy **25**

Game 2: Ziggy at the Market **37**

Game 3: Treasure Hunt with Ziggy **47**

Game 4: Ziggy Teaches School **57**

Game 5: Ziggy at the Beach **65**

Game 6: Caving with Ziggy **75**

Game 7: Ziggy Rounds Up Horses **87**

Game 8: Ziggy Plays with Penguins **97**

Game 9: Blast Off with Ziggy! **109**

1
Preparing for Takeoff

Correlation with All About Reading Level 1

The games included in *Reading Games with Ziggy the Zebra* are a fun way for children to review the concepts in *All About Reading* Level 1. The chart below outlines when each game is mentioned in the Level 1 Teacher's Manual.

Beginning in this lesson	Play this game	Purpose
Lesson 1	Apples for Ziggy	Recognize vowels and consonants
Lesson 2	Ziggy at the Market	Practice Phonogram Cards
Lesson 3	Ziggy at the Beach	Practice Word Cards
Lesson 4	Treasure Hunt with Ziggy	Reinforce that every word has a vowel
Lesson 6	Ziggy Teaches School	Practice with blending
Lesson 19	Caving with Ziggy	Practice Phonogram and Word Cards
Lesson 33	Ziggy Rounds Up Horses	Practice Phonogram and Word Cards
Lesson 44	Ziggy Plays with Penguins	Practice Phonogram Cards
Lesson 50	Blast Off with Ziggy!	Practice counting syllables

Meet Ziggy!

If you used the *All About Reading* Pre-reading program, the Zigzag Zebra needs no introduction. But if you are new to our reading series...then meet Ziggy!

Ziggy is a young zebra who is learning to read right along with your students. He is a supportive friend for beginning readers, and he likes to have a good time as he learns. In the Pre-reading program, Ziggy is represented by a plush puppet, but if you do not own a Ziggy puppet, don't despair! Make a stand-up Ziggy using a file folder and the graphic of Ziggy on the next page.

❶ Remove Ziggy from page 11 and trim edges as needed. Glue to the front of a file folder.

❷ Whenever you play a game, just prop up Ziggy so he can play along!

Map of Ziggy's Travels

Ziggy will be traveling to nine different areas of the world as he and your student practice reading skills. Your student can follow along by locating each country as it is visited.

Prepare the Map

1. Remove the map on pages 14 and 15 and trim edges as needed. Glue the two-page spread inside a file folder as shown here.

2. Remove the cover sheet on page 17. Attach this sheet to the front of the file folder.

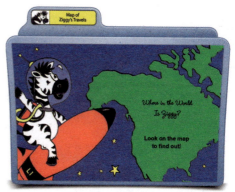

3. Cut out the label on page 17. Glue the label onto the file folder tab.

Ziggy's Destination Guide

Ziggy is a globe trotter! Your student will have fun traveling to these parts of the world:

- » Washington, United States of America in "Apples for Ziggy"
- » Paris, France in "Ziggy at the Market"
- » Caribbean Island in "Treasure Hunt with Ziggy"
- » New Zealand in "Ziggy Teaches School"
- » Capetown, South Africa in "Ziggy at the Beach"
- » Argentina, South America in "Caving with Ziggy"
- » Mongolia, Asia in "Ziggy Rounds Up Horses"
- » South Pole, Antarctica in "Ziggy Plays with Penguins"
- » Outer Space in "Blast Off with Ziggy!"

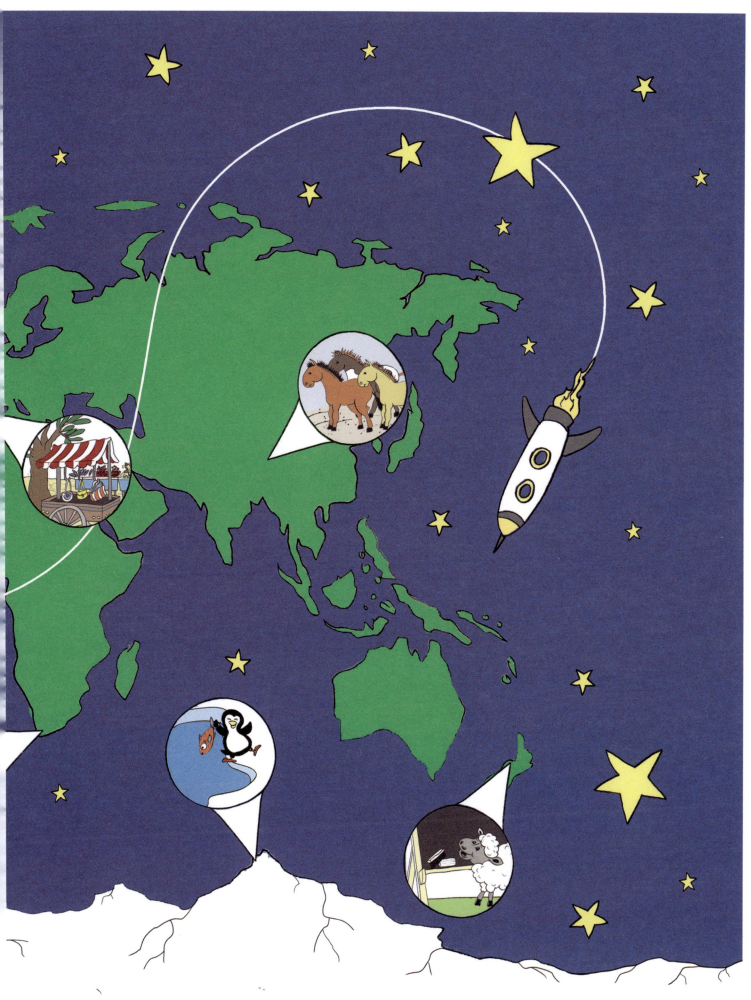

Map of Ziggy's Travels

How to Make the File Folder Games

Materials
- » 10 file folders
- » Scissors
- » Glue stick or rubber cement
- » Tape

Assembly

❶ Remove the desired game board from the book and trim edges as needed. Glue the two-page spread inside a file folder.

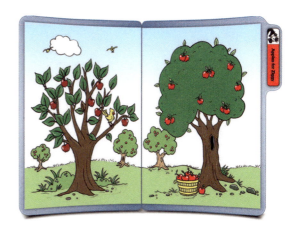

❷ Cut out the corresponding pocket. Attach the pocket to the front of the file folder by taping on three sides, leaving the top open. Use this pocket to store the instructions and game pieces.

❸ Cut out the label and glue onto the file folder tab.

❹ Cut out the game pieces and store them in the pocket.

Storage Ideas

Keep your file folder games in one of these places:
- » file drawer
- » between two bookends on a book shelf
- » plastic storage crate
- » Ziploc® bags
- » box

Who Goes First?

Most of the games in *Reading Games with Ziggy the Zebra* are designed for two players—either Ziggy and the child or two children. Of course, you can play the part of Ziggy! So how do you decide who goes first?

Try some of the following fun possibilities.

- » Show a Word or Phonogram Card to the players. Whoever says the correct word or sound first gets to go first.

- » Think of a number from 1 to 10. Whoever guesses the number, or closest to it, goes first.

- » Play Rock-Paper-Scissors.

- » Have each player roll the dice. Whoever has the highest number goes first.

- » Draw straws. Whoever draws the longest straw goes first.

- » Play Eeny-Meeny-Miney-Mo.

2
Up and Away!

Assembly

❶ Remove the game board on pages 26 and 27 and trim edges as needed. Glue the two-page spread inside the file folder.

❷ Cut out the pocket on page 29. Attach the pocket to the front of the file folder by taping on three sides, leaving the top open. Use this pocket to store the instructions and game pieces.

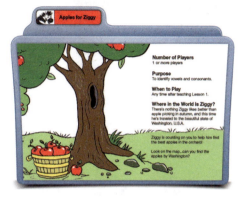

❸ Cut out the label on page 29 and glue onto the file folder tab.

❹ Cut out the game pieces on pages 31 and 33 and store them in the pocket.

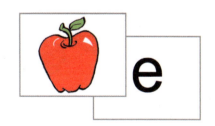

Apples for Ziggy

Number of Players
1 or more players

Purpose
To identify vowels and consonants.

When to Play
Any time after teaching Lesson 1.

Where in the World Is Ziggy?
There's nothing Ziggy likes better than apple picking in autumn, and this time he's traveled to the beautiful state of **Washington, U.S.A.**

Ziggy is counting on you to help him find the best apples in the orchard!

Look on the map…can you find the apples by Washington?

Game 1: Apples for Ziggy

Play Instructions

Game setup

❶ Shuffle the apple game pieces and arrange 24 of them on the trees with the apples facing up. The game pieces may overlap. Place the remaining 24 game pieces in a draw pile to refill the trees later.

❷ If only one child is available to play, Ziggy can be the other player.

Quick review before playing

Discuss the words *consonant* and *vowel* with your child. Refresh his or her memory by repeating the vowels: "a, e, i, o, u, and sometimes y."

How to play

✱ **Take out the Ziggy Zebra puppet and put it on. Ziggy says:**

"I'm visiting the state of Washington, and I've discovered an orchard filled with apple trees! I love apples and can't wait to try some…but today, I am particularly hungry for apples with vowels on them."

"Can you help me find some apples to eat?"

"Pick four apples from these trees." *Child picks the apples.*

"Now flip over the apples!" *Child turns over each apple to reveal the letter.*

"Are there any vowels?" *Child says the names of the vowels, if any. The child then keeps the game pieces with vowels on them.*

✱ **Place the consonant pieces in a discard pile. Take four new apples from the draw pile and place them on the tree.**

(continued…)

"Now, it's ____'s turn."

❋ **Play continues with the next player or, if only one child, with Ziggy.**

Game continues until all apples in the draw pile have been used.

Who wins?

The winner is the player with the most vowels. At the end of the game, the winner gets to feed his or her collection of "vowel apples" to Ziggy.

For a shorter game

Don't replenish the apples on the trees after each turn.

Store these instructions in the pocket on the front of the file folder game.

Ziggy at the Market

Assembly

① Remove the game board on pages 38 and 39 and trim edges as needed. Glue the two-page spread inside the file folder.

② Cut out the pocket on page 41. Attach the pocket to the front of the file folder by taping on three sides, leaving the top open. Use this pocket to store the instructions and game pieces.

③ Cut out the label on page 41 and glue onto the file folder tab.

④ Cut out the game pieces on page 43 and store them in the pocket.

You're ready to play!

Ziggy at the Market ← Label

↳ Pocket for front of file folder

Number of Players
1 or more players

Purpose
To identify Phonogram Cards.

When to Play
Any time after teaching Lesson 2.

Where in the World Is Ziggy?
Ziggy is a very fashionable zebra, and he likes to shop almost as much as he likes to read. One of his favorite places to shop is **Paris, France**, where he can find all sorts of stylish things. Maybe you can help him find just the right *chapeau* (hat) — preferably with a feather in it!

Look on the map...can you find the market cart by Paris, France?

Reading Games with Ziggy the Zebra

Game 2: Ziggy at the Market

Play Instructions

Game setup

❶ Stack all the hats on one basket on the game board, all the flowers on another basket, and so on.

❷ Select the Phonogram Cards from behind the child's Review divider. Each child will have his or her own pile of Phonogram Cards, according to what he or she needs to review. If Ziggy is one of the players, he can use a stack of cards from behind the Mastered divider.

❸ In pencil, lightly write a number (1, 2, or 3) in the corner on the front of each Phonogram Card, or use a small Post-It® Note to attach a number to the card. This number will represent the number of items the child can buy at the market when the card is drawn.

❹ If only one child is available to play, Ziggy can be the other player.

How to play

✺ **Take out the Ziggy Zebra puppet and put it on. Ziggy says:**

"I'm going shopping at an open-air market in Paris, France. There are so many wonderful things to buy!"

"Today I'm shopping for hats, bananas, flowers, shoes, and pots and pans. Will you help me with my shopping, please?"

"As we walk up and down the streets of Paris, we can review some of our Phonogram Cards! We can each practice our own cards while we shop."

✺ **The first player begins by drawing a Phonogram Card and saying the sound(s).**

(continued...)

❋ **The player looks at the number on the card, and then "purchases" that number of items from the baskets on the game board.**

The Phonogram Card is returned to the bottom of the player's pile.

"Now, it's ____'s turn."

❋ **Play continues with the next player or, if only one child, with Ziggy.**

Game continues until all game cards in the draw pile have been used.

Who wins?
The winner is the player with the most purchased items.

> *Store these instructions in the pocket on the front of the file folder game.*

Treasure Hunt with Ziggy

Assembly

❶ Remove the game board on pages 48 and 49 and trim edges as needed. Glue the two-page spread inside the file folder.

❷ Cut out the pocket on page 51. Attach the pocket to the front of the file folder by taping on three sides, leaving the top open. Use this pocket to store the instructions and game pieces.

❸ Cut out the label on page 51 and glue onto the file folder tab.

❹ Cut out the game pieces on page 53 and store them in the pocket.

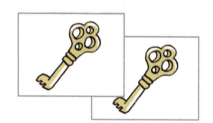

You're ready to play!

© 2016 by All About® Learning Press, Inc.

Treasure Hunt with Ziggy

Number of Players
1 player

Purpose
To reinforce the concept that every word must have a vowel.

When to Play
Any time after teaching Lesson 3.

Where in the World Is Ziggy?
Did you know zebras are experts at scuba diving? That's one of Ziggy's favorite pastimes, so he's always glad when he goes on another trip to the **Caribbean islands**. The sea is full of shipwrecks to explore, so put on your goggles and go diving for treasure with Ziggy!

Look on the map...can you find the treasure chest by the Caribbean islands?

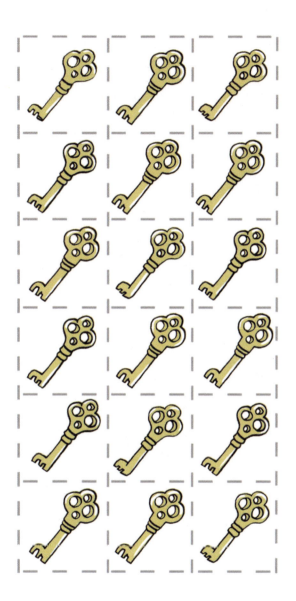

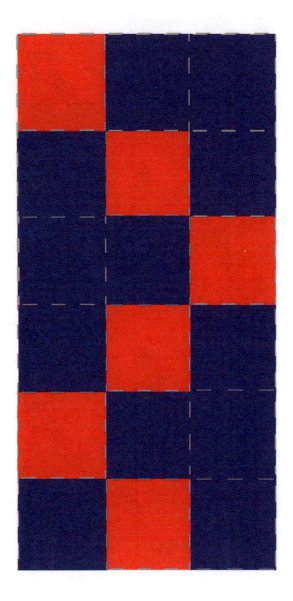

Game 3: Treasure Hunt with Ziggy

Play Instructions

Game setup

❶ Place the game pieces in a pile on the game board, with keys facing up.

❷ Gather 12 pennies, M&M candies, or other small goodies to use as "treasure." Place some treasure on the game board below each chest.

Quick Review Before Playing

Look at the letter tile setup on your magnet board with your child. Review the facts that consonants are blue and vowels are red, and that every word must have at least one vowel.

How to Play

✸ **Take out the Ziggy Zebra puppet and put it on. Ziggy says:**

"I was exploring a remote island in the Caribbean, and I found six treasure chests! All of the chests are locked, and I need your help to unlock them. I think there may be treasure inside!"

"Which treasure chest should we try to unlock first?" *Child chooses.*

"Choose three keys from the pile. Set one key over each lock on the treasure chest."

"Now flip over the keys!"

"Could this be a word?"

(continued...)

Which Combinations Open the Locks?

Red tiles are vowels and blue tiles are consonants.

If your child draws these combinations, the locks will open:
- ONE red tile and TWO blue tiles (e.g., mat, beg)
- TWO red tiles and ONE blue tile (e.g., see, ate)

The red tiles can be in any position.

If your child draws three red tiles or three blue tiles, the locks will not open because the combination cannot be a word.

✸ **If your child draws a correct combination of keys, the chest will be "unlocked" and the child gets the treasure you placed below it.**

If the combination of keys your child chooses does *not* unlock the chest, he or she can try again.

Return the keys to the draw pile after each attempt.

TIP!

These examples of three-letter words show that the vowel can be in any position:

       end   try   bat   eat   bee

Game continues until all the chests have been unlocked and the treasure distributed.

Store these instructions in the pocket on the front of the file folder game.

Ziggy Teaches School

Assembly

① Remove the game board on pages 58 and 59 and trim edges as needed. Glue the two-page spread inside the file folder.

② Cut out the pocket on page 61. Attach the pocket to the front of the file folder by taping on three sides, leaving the top open. Use this pocket to store the instructions and game pieces.

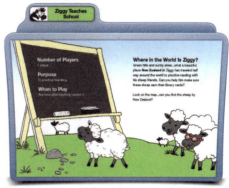

③ Cut out the label on page 61 and glue onto the file folder tab.

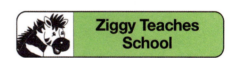

You're ready to play!

© 2016 by All About® Learning Press, Inc.   *Reading Games with Ziggy the Zebra*

← Pocket for front of file folder

Where in the World Is Ziggy?

Green hills and sunny skies…what a beautiful place **New Zealand** is! Ziggy has traveled half way around the world to practice reading with his sheep friends. Can you help him make sure these sheep earn their library cards?

Look on the map…can you find the sheep by New Zealand?

← Label

Ziggy Teaches School

Number of Players
1 player

Purpose
To practice blending.

When to Play
Any time after teaching Lesson 4.

© 2016 by All About® Learning Press, Inc. *Reading Games with Ziggy the Zebra* **61**

Game 4: Ziggy Teaches School

Play Instructions

Game setup

❶ Gather a selection of Word Cards from behind the child's Review divider. These are the words that you will build with letter tiles during the game.

❷ From your magnet board, gather the letter tiles you'll need to spell the chosen Word Cards.

How to play

✱ **Take out the Ziggy Zebra puppet and put it on. Ziggy says:**

"I'm on the island of New Zealand in the South Pacific, and look how many sheep have come to my school!"

"These sheep would like to learn how to read, but I'm still learning myself. Can you help me teach the sheep to read?" *Child says yes.*

✱ **Using the letter tiles, form a word on Ziggy's blackboard by setting out one letter at a time. Your child will say the sound of each letter as it is set out.**

After your child says each sound, have Ziggy read the entire word aloud. Occasionally, have Ziggy get the word wrong, and allow your child to correct the mistake: *No, Ziggy, c-u-t isn't cup, it's cut!*

After each word is read, your child can "erase" Ziggy's blackboard by removing the letter tiles.

Game continues until all the selected Word Cards have been spelled and read on the game board.

Store these instructions in the pocket on the front of the file folder game.

Ziggy at the Beach

Assembly

❶ Remove the game board on pages 66 and 67 and trim edges as needed. Glue the two-page spread inside the file folder.

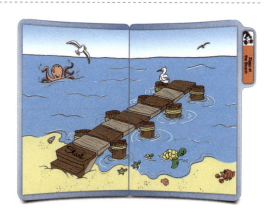

❷ Cut out the pocket on page 69. Attach the pocket to the front of the file folder by taping on three sides, leaving the top open. Use this pocket to store the instructions and game pieces.

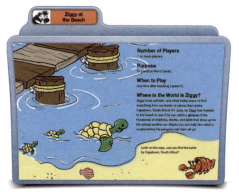

❸ Cut out the label on page 69 and glue onto the file folder tab.

❹ Cut out the game pieces on page 71 and store them in the pocket.

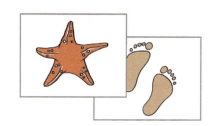

You're ready to play!

Ziggy at the Beach

Number of Players
1 or more players

Purpose
To practice Word Cards.

When to Play
Any time after teaching Lesson 5.

Where in the World Is Ziggy?
Ziggy loves animals—and what better place to find everything from aardvarks to zebras than sunny **Capetown, South Africa!** It's June, so Ziggy has headed to the beach to see if he can catch a glimpse of the thousands of dolphins, sharks, and birds that show up for the annual sardine run. Maybe you can help him catch a couple before the penguins eat them all up!

Look on the map...can you find the turtle by Capetown, South Africa?

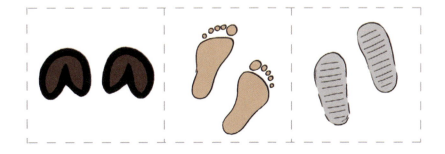

71

Game 5: Ziggy at the Beach

Play Instructions

Game setup

❶ Arrange the starfish game pieces in the water around the pier. Put one set of footprints for each player on the START space.

❷ Select the Word Cards from behind the child's Review divider. Each child will have his or her own pile of Word Cards, according to what he or she needs to review. If Ziggy is one of the players, he can use a stack of cards from behind the Mastered divider.

❸ In pencil, lightly write a number (2, 3, or 4) in the corner on the front of each Word Card, or use a small Post-It® Note to attach a number to the card. This number will represent the number of spaces the player can move forward when the card is drawn.

❹ If only one child is available to play, Ziggy can be the other player.

How to play

✳ **Take out the Ziggy Zebra puppet and put it on. Ziggy says:**

"Look! I'm enjoying the sunshine on the beaches of Capetown, South Africa! Would you like to play on the beach with me?"

"I want to collect starfish today, so let's play a game where we run to the end of the pier, jump in the ocean, and see who can gather the most starfish!"

"But before we can collect starfish, let's review some of our Word Cards. We can each practice our own cards while we play on the pier."

✳ **The first player draws a Word Card from the top of his or her pile and reads the word aloud. If the word is read correctly, the player can move the footprints ahead the number of spaces indicated on the card.**

(continued...)

❋ **If the word is read incorrectly, coach the child through the blending procedure as outlined in Appendix C of the** *All About Reading* **Level 1 Teacher's Manual.**

Return the Word Card to the bottom of the player's pile.

"Now, it's ___'s turn."

❋ **Play continues with the next player or, if only one child, with Ziggy.**

When players draw a card that allows them to run off the pier, they can collect a starfish and add it to their own pile. They then set their footprints back on the START space.

Game continues until all the starfish have been collected.

Who wins?
Everyone who jumps in the ocean and finds a starfish!

Store these instructions in the pocket on the front of the file folder game.

Caving with Ziggy

Assembly

① Remove the game board on pages 76 and 77 and trim edges as needed. Glue the two-page spread inside the file folder.

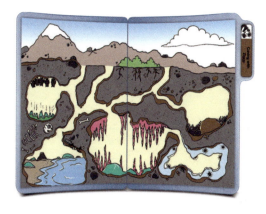

② Cut out the pocket on page 79. Attach the pocket to the front of the file folder by taping on three sides, leaving the top open. Use this pocket to store the instructions and game pieces.

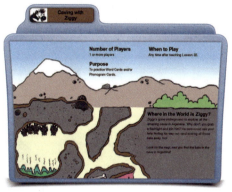

③ Cut out the label on page 79 and glue onto the file folder tab.

④ Cut out the game pieces on page 81 and store them in the pocket. Remove the backpack graphic on page 83 and store it in the file folder.

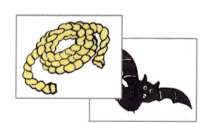

You're ready to play!

© 2016 by All About® Learning Press, Inc. Reading Games with Ziggy the Zebra

← Label

← Pocket for front of file folder

Caving with Ziggy

When to Play
Any time after teaching Lesson 17.

Number of Players
1 or more players

Purpose
To practice Word Cards and/or Phonogram Cards.

Where in the World Is Ziggy?
Ziggy's gone underground to explore all the amazing caves in **Argentina**. Why don't you grab a flashlight and join him? He sure could use your help finding his way out—and scaring all those bats away, too!

Look on the map…can you find the bats in the cave in Argentina?

© 2016 by All About® Learning Press, Inc.   *Reading Games with Ziggy the Zebra*   79

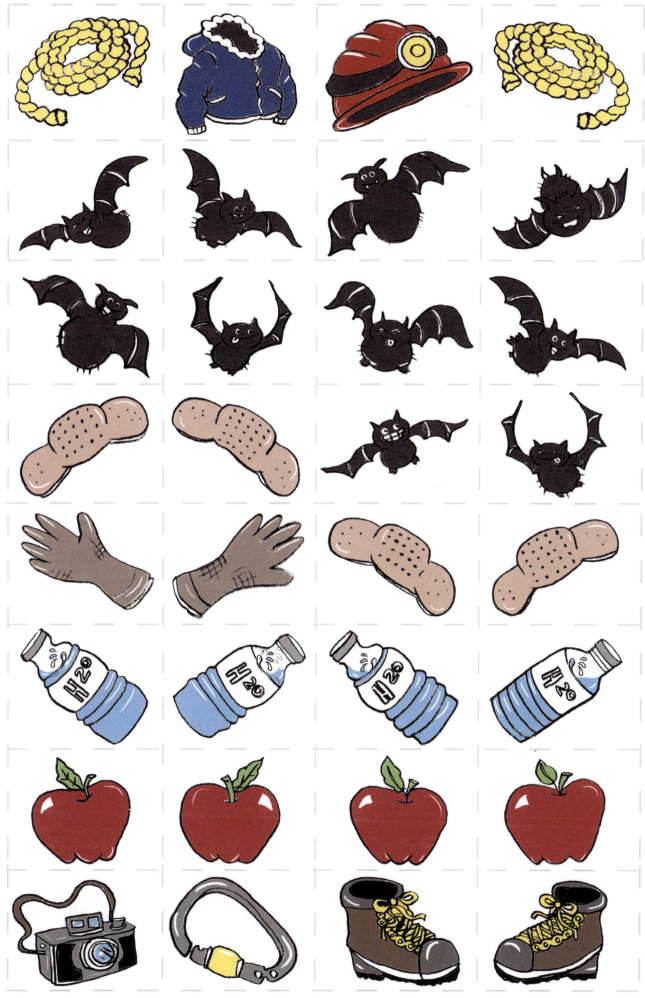

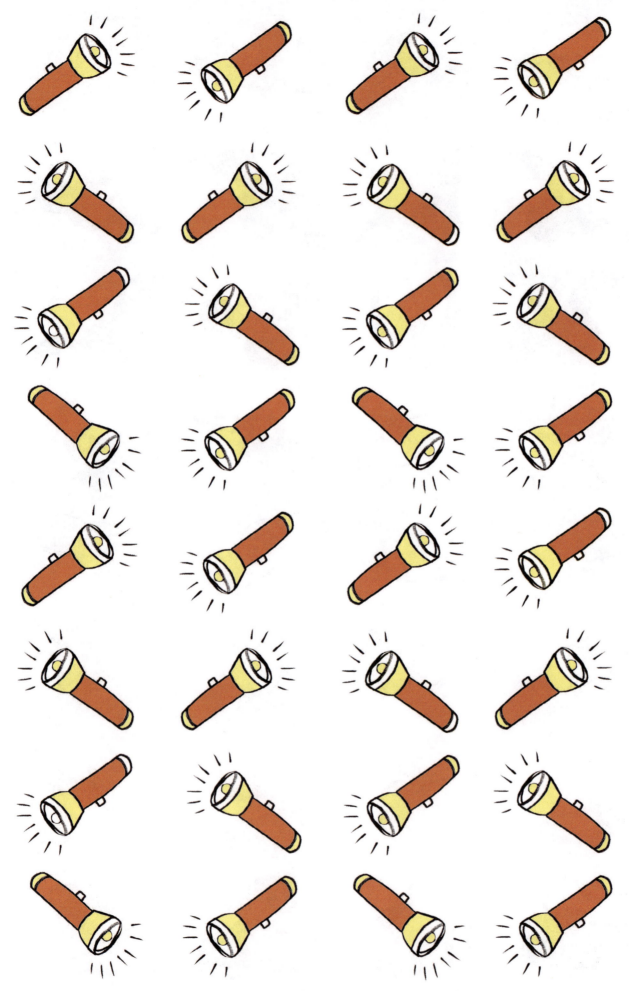

Game 6: Caving with Ziggy

Play Instructions

Game setup

❶ Distribute the game pieces around the caves on the game board with the flashlights facing up.

❷ Set the backpack page next to the game board.

❸ Select the Word Cards or Phonogram Cards from behind the child's Review divider. Each child will have his or her own pile of cards, according to what he or she needs to review. If Ziggy is one of the players, he can use a stack of cards from behind the Mastered divider.

❹ If only one child is available to play, Ziggy can be the other player.

How to play

✳ **Take out the Ziggy Zebra puppet and put it on. Ziggy says:**

"I've been exploring a cave in Argentina, but I didn't realize that my backpack was open. All my caving equipment has fallen out of my backpack! Will you explore the cave with me to help me find the missing items?"

"Wonderful!"

"Now, take a card from your pile and read the word (or say the sound) aloud." *Child reads the word or says the sound of the phonogram.*

✳ **If the player answers correctly, Ziggy says:**

"That's right! Now you can retrieve one of my lost items from the cave. Select a card and turn it over. Is it one of my lost items? Then go ahead and put it in my backpack! Thanks!"

(continued...)

❋ **The player places the lost item "in" the backpack by putting the card under the backpack sheet.**

If the player reads the word or says the sound incorrectly, Ziggy can guide the child as needed.

If the player selects a game piece that features a bat, leave the card in the cave, face up.

Return the Word or Phonogram Card to the bottom of the player's pile.

"Now, it's ____'s turn."

❋ **Play continues with the next player or, if only one child, with Ziggy.**

Game continues until all the lost caving equipment has been retrieved and placed in Ziggy's backpack.

Who wins?
Everyone who finds an item and adds it to Ziggy's backpack!

For a shorter game
Don't place all of the bats in the cave.

Store these instructions in the pocket on the front of the file folder game.

Ziggy Rounds Up Horses

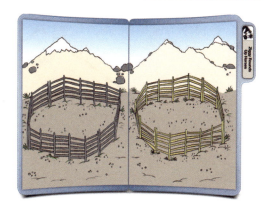

Assembly

1. Remove the game board on pages 88 and 89 and trim edges as needed. Glue the two-page spread inside the file folder.

2. Cut out the pocket on page 91. Attach the pocket to the front of the file folder by taping on three sides, leaving the top open. Use this pocket to store the instructions and game pieces.

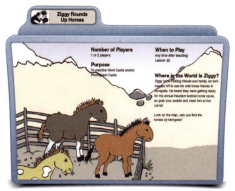

3. Cut out the label on page 91 and glue onto the file folder tab.

4. Cut out the game pieces on page 93 and store them in the pocket.

You're ready to play!

Ziggy Rounds Up Horses

← Label

↓ Pocket for front of file folder

Number of Players
1 or 2 players

Purpose
To practice Word Cards and/or Phonogram Cards.

When to Play
Any time after teaching Lesson 32.

Where in the World Is Ziggy?
Ziggy loves visiting friends and family, so he's headed off to see his wild horse friends in **Mongolia**. He heard they were getting ready for the annual Naadam festival horse races, so grab your saddle and meet him at the corral!

Look on the map…can you find the horses by Mongolia?

© 2016 by All About® Learning Press, Inc. Reading Games with Ziggy the Zebra

Game 7: Ziggy Rounds Up Horses

Play Instructions

Game setup

① Arrange the game pieces around the perimeter of the game board with the hoofprints facing up.

② Assign one corral to each player.

③ Select the Word Cards or Phonogram Cards from behind the child's Review divider. Each child will have his or her own pile of cards, according to what he or she needs to review. If Ziggy is one of the players, he can use a stack of cards from behind the Mastered divider.

④ If only one child is available to play, Ziggy can be the other player.

How to play

❋ **Take out the Ziggy Zebra puppet and put it on. Ziggy says:**

"I'm having a marvelous adventure in Asia. Today I'm helping to move wild horses from the grassy plains of Mongolia and into corrals! But these horses are frisky and full of energy. Can you help me move the horses?"

"I like to make noise while I round up the horses—you can, too! Yee haw! Whoa!"

❋ **The first player selects a game card and flips it over. If the player reveals a horse card, then the player chooses a Word or Phonogram Card and reads it aloud. If the card is read correctly, the player places the horse card in his or her corral.**

If the card is read incorrectly, the player can try again.

Return the Word or Phonogram Card to the bottom of the player's pile.

(continued...)

❇ If the player reveals a broken fence card, it means that a horse has escaped from the corral. In this case, the player does not read a Word or Phonogram Card; instead, the player must move one of his or her horses out of the corral and back onto the grassy plains around the edge of the gameboard. Leave the broken fence card face up on the perimeter of the game board.

"Now, it's ____'s turn."

❇ Play continues with the next player or, if only one child, with Ziggy.

Game continues until all the horses have been moved into the corrals. Each player can count the number of horses in his or her corral.

Who wins?
The winner is the player with the most horses in his or her corral.

> Store these instructions in the pocket on the front of the file folder game.

Ziggy Plays with Penguins

Assembly

① Remove the game board on pages 98 and 99 and trim edges as needed. Glue the two-page spread inside the file folder.

② Cut out the pocket on page 101. Attach the pocket to the front of the file folder by taping on three sides, leaving the top open. Use this pocket to store the instructions and game pieces.

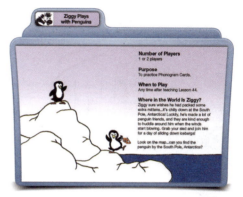

③ Cut out the label on page 101 and glue onto the file folder tab.

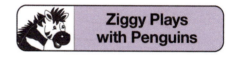

④ Cut out the game pieces on pages 103 and 105 and store them in the pocket.

You're ready to play!

Ziggy Plays with Penguins

Number of Players
1 or 2 players

Purpose
To practice Phonogram Cards.

When to Play
Any time after teaching Lesson 44.

Where in the World Is Ziggy?
Ziggy sure wishes he had packed some extra mittens...it's chilly down at the **South Pole, Antarctica!** Luckily, he's made a lot of penguin friends, and they are kind enough to huddle around him when the winds start blowing. Grab your sled and join him for a day of sliding down icebergs!

Look on the map...can you find the penguin by the South Pole, Antarctica?

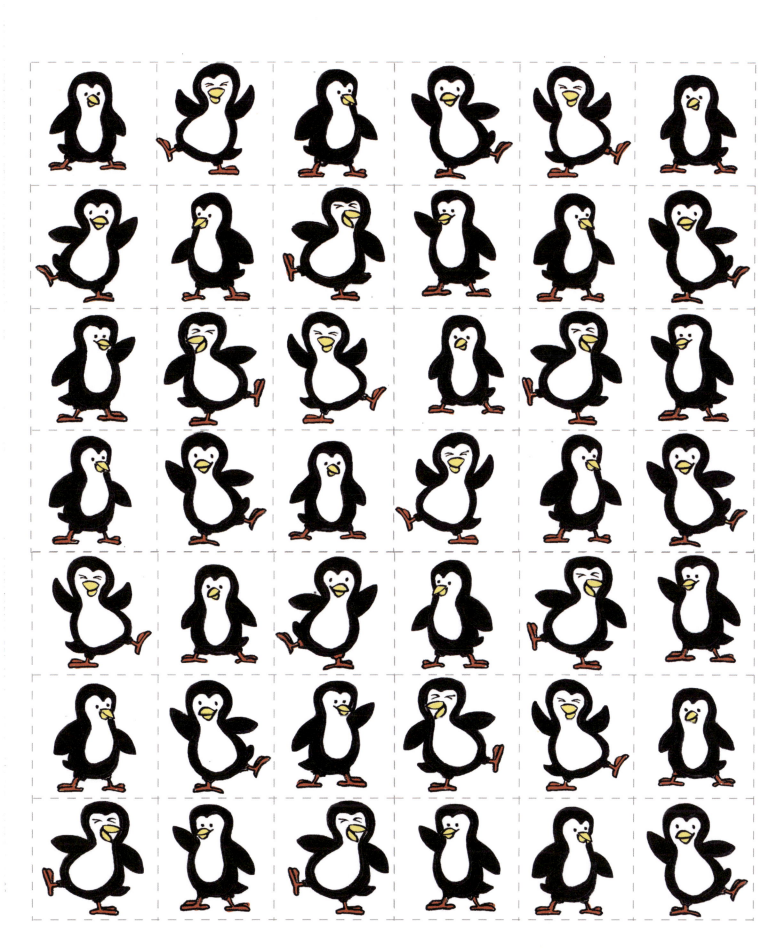

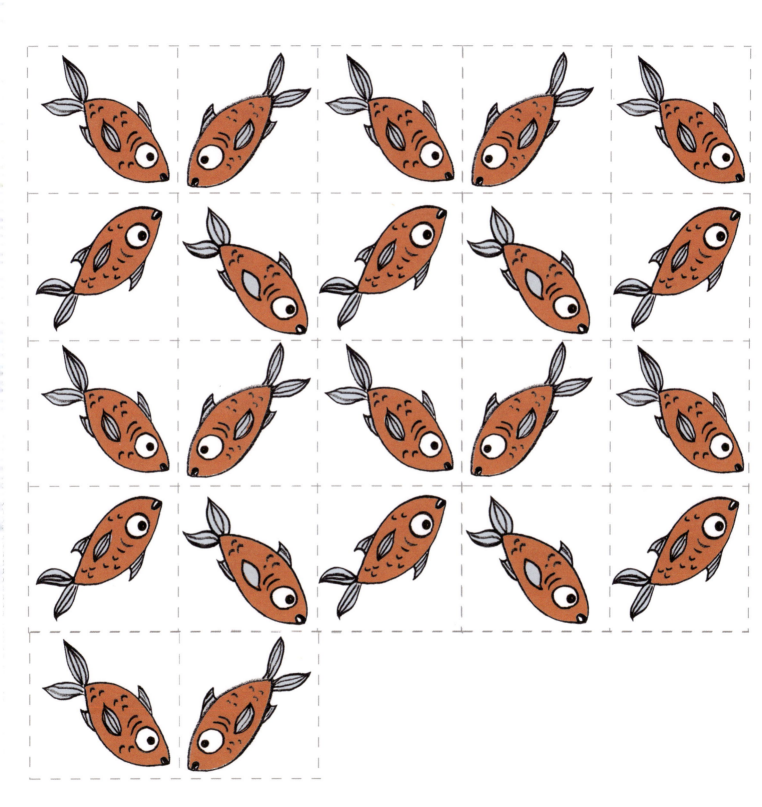

b d p s t

v w x th sh

ck ng nk a i

c o g e u

y ch

Game 8: Ziggy Plays with Penguins

Play Instructions

Game setup

❶ Place the stack of penguin game pieces face up at the top of the iceberg. Place the stack of fish game pieces face up at the bottom of the game board.

❷ Assign one pool of water to each player.

❸ If only one child is available to play, Ziggy can be the other player.

How to play

✸ **Take out the Ziggy Zebra puppet and put it on. Ziggy says:**

"I'm visiting the South Pole in Antarctica! I've seen so many beautiful penguins, including Emperor penguins, Adélie penguins, Chinstrap penguins, and Gentoo penguins."

"All of the penguins are at the top of this amazing iceberg. The penguins want to slide down into the pools, but they need our help!"

✸ **The first player draws a fish card and flips it over to reveal a phonogram. The player says all of the sounds the phonogram makes. If it makes one sound, the player helps one penguin slide down the iceberg into the player's pool of water. If the phonogram makes two sounds, the player helps two penguins slide into the water, and so on.**

"Now, it's ____'s turn."

✸ **Play continues with the next player or, if only one child, with Ziggy.**

Game continues until all the penguins have slid into the water. Each player can count the number of penguins in his or her pool of water.

(continued...)

Who wins?

The winner is the player with the most penguins in his or her pool.

> **TIP!**
>
> In Lesson 44, use these fish cards: **b, d, p, s, t, v, w, x, th, sh, ck, ng, nk, a, i, c**
>
> After Lesson 45, add in these fish cards: **o, g**
>
> After Lesson 46, add in these fish cards: **e, u, y, ch**

Store these instructions in the pocket on the front of the file folder game.

Blast Off with Ziggy!

Assembly

❶ Remove the game board on pages 110 and 111 and trim edges as needed. Glue the two-page spread inside the file folder.

❷ Cut out the pocket on page 113. Attach the pocket to the front of the file folder by taping on three sides, leaving the top open. Use this pocket to store the instructions and game pieces.

❸ Cut out the label on page 113 and glue onto the file folder tab.

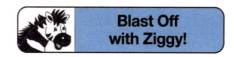

❹ Cut out the game pieces on pages 115 and 117 and store them in the pocket.

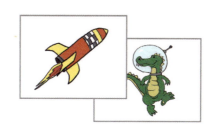

You're ready to play!

Blast Off with Ziggy!

Number of Players
1 or more players

Purpose
To practice counting syllables.

When to Play
Any time after teaching Lesson 47.

Where in the World Is Ziggy?
Ziggy is on the most amazing journey of his life! He's zooming past stars and meteors and galaxies, just a little zebra in the vastness of **outer space.** Put on your spacesuit—it's time to soar over the moon!

Look on the map...can you find the rocket in outer space?

Game 9: Blast Off with Ziggy!

Play Instructions

Game setup

❶ Place the stack of game pieces at the bottom of the game board. Place the players' spaceship markers on the START space.

❷ If only one child is available to play, Ziggy can be the other player.

How to play

✳ **Take out the Ziggy Zebra puppet and put it on. Ziggy says:**

"I've traveled the world and visited all seven continents, but now I'm exploring outer space!"

"Let's fly off to Saturn, a large planet with many rings. Come with me—hop on the puffs of smoke from my rocket!"

✳ **The first player draws a game card and flips it over. The player looks at the picture on the card and determines the number of syllables in that word. The player then advances his or her marker one space for each syllable in the word.**

Return the game card to the bottom of the pile.

"Now, it's ____'s turn."

✳ **Play continues with the next player or, if only one child, with Ziggy.**

Game continues until all the spaceships have reached the FINISH space and all the players are on Saturn.

Who wins?

Everyone who gets safely to Saturn!

Store these instructions in the pocket on the front of the file folder game.